# FUGITIVE SLAVE LAW.

THE

# Religious Duty

OF

# OBEDIENCE TO LAW:

A

# SERMON,

Preached in the Second Presbyterian Church

IN BROOKLYN, NOV. 24, 1850.

BY ICHABOD S. SPENCER, D.D.

NEW YORK:
PUBLISHED BY M. W. DODD,
BRICK CHURCH CHAPEL, CITY HALL SQUARE,
OPPOSITE THE CITY HALL.
1850.

TO THE REV. DR. SPENCER:

The undersigned having listened, with much pleasure and as we hope profit, to the Sermon which you delivered yesterday morning, most respectfully request a copy of the same for publication, believing that much good may be done to the cause of Religion and Law, by the dissemination of the truths expressed therein.

*Brooklyn, Monday, Nov.* 25, 1850.

JASPER CORNING,
FRANCIS H. ABBOTT,
LEBBEUS CHAPMAN,
F. DEMING,
GEORGE A. TALBOT,
A. M. FENBY,
THOMAS COCHRAN,
WM. BARBOUR,
J. B. WICKHAM,
SAMUEL HUTCHINSON,
WM. H. AMES,
L. HOPKINS,
JARVIS BRUSH,
S. N. BROWN,
GEORGE P. LORD,
H. K. CORNING,
THOS. BAYLIS,
W. K. BROWN,
M. S. GOODMAN,
JAS. WILDE, JR.,
GEO. A. TOWNSEND,
DAVID B. BAYLIS,
HENRY W. BARNES,
ELI MERRILL,
W. M. SANDS,
ISAAC OTIS,
ALANSON TRASK,
CHARLES CLARK,
JOHN T. LAWRENCE,
A. S. MARVIN,
WM. M. HARRIS,
R. R. FIELD,
SAMUEL T. HUBBARD,
RICHARD W. HUBBARD,
A. G. TRASK,
JOHN H. PRENTICE,
WALDO HUTCHINS,
E. L. BUSHNELL,
SUMNER STONE,
JOSEPH STEELE,
JAS. McLEAN,
J. C. MEEKER,
J. S. PIERSON,
A. G. JENNINGS, JR.,
B. W. DELAMATER,
W. SPENCER,
J. C. DURYEA,
A. CRITTENDEN,
HENRY ROWLAND,
WM. BULLARD,
JN. BULLARD, JR.

---

TO JASPER CORNING, ESQ., AND OTHERS:

GENTLEMEN—The sermon which you have requested, prepared without a single thought of its publication, and amid a pressure of other duties, I submit to your disposal;—governed more by your judgment than my own, in reference to its fitness for the press.

Yours, very truly,

I. S. SPENCER.

*Brooklyn, Nov.* 26, 1850.

# SERMON.

Titus, III. 1. Put them in mind to be subject to principalities and powers, to obey magistrates, to be ready for every good work.

Ro. xiii. 1-7. Let every soul be subject unto the higher powers. For there is no power but of God, the powers that be, are ordained of God. Whosoever, therefore, resisteth the power, resisteth the ordinance of God, and they that resist shall receive to themselves damnation: (harm, loss, or ruin). For rulers are not a terror to good works, but to the evil. Wilt thou then not be afraid of the power? do that which is good and thou shalt have praise of the same: for he is the minister of God to thee for good. But if thou do that which is evil, be afraid; for he beareth not the sword in vain: for he is the minister of God, a revenger to execute wrath upon him that doeth evil. Wherefore ye must needs be subject, not only for wrath, but also for conscience' sake. For, for this cause pay ye tribute also, for they are God's ministers, attending continually upon this very thing. Render therefore to all their dues: tribute to whom tribute is due; custom to whom custom; fear to whom fear; honor to whom honor.

There are two great classes of human duty. One of them embraces duties which we owe to God, the other embraces duties which we owe to men.

This classification of duties received the sanction of Jesus Christ, when he spake of *loving the Lord our God with all our heart*, as the spirit and sum of the one class of duties, and of *loving our neighbor as ourselves*, as the spirit and sum of the other class of duties. It had also been previously taught at Mount Sinai, when God gave to Moses the two tables of the law—the one enjoining our duty to God, the other enjoining our duty to man.

This classification of duties is not arbitrary. It is founded on truth and nature. Men have relations to God, as their Creator, Upholder, Governor, Redeemer, and rightful Judge; and they are bound to recognize these relations, and feel and act accordingly. Men hold relations to one another, as parents, children, citizens, rulers, and subjects; and they are bound to recognize these relations, and feel and act accordingly. Such is the will of God. Such is the law of God. There can be no holiness in man aside from conformity to the will of God in this thing.

This principle is carried out in all the teachings of the New Testament, with an emphasis and a plainness which no candid and unprejudiced mind can fail to understand. Jesus Christ has incorporated it into his sermon on the mount in many particulars, wherein he insists upon our social duties, while he teaches religion. He preached this principle when he said, "render unto Cæsar the things that are Cæsar's, and unto God the things that are God's." He practised on this principle when he made the fish bring in his mouth the tribute-money which, as a citizen, he owed to the government of the country,—a government a thousand-fold more oppressive than ours.

It would be a fundamental error, if we were to maintain, that *religion* has nothing to do with the regulation of our conduct towards one another,—as parents, as children, as magistrates, subjects and citizens; but that it has left all that field of duty to be regulated by the individual preferences of men. It has not done so. Social duties come as really within the field of *religious* obligation, as any other duties. "The fifth commandment requireth the preserving the honor and performing the duties belonging to every one in their several places and relations, as superiors, inferiors, and equals." As men, in any relationship we hold, neighbors, citizens of the state, children, parents, or any other earthly connection, religion extends its authority over us; and our conduct in each one of these relationships constitutes a part of our holiness or our sin.

God has not seen fit to enact special or particular laws for us, to regulate our conduct in all respects, as here associated with one another, and owing duties to one another, as neighbors, citizens of the commonwealth, husbands, wives, and children. He has himself enacted only *general* laws for us,—laid down great general principles, under the authority and light of which, he has left men to regulate the particulars as they please, by the governments which they establish,—only not contravening his great general principles and laws.

He has himself made *all* the laws which are needful, and all which can be justly obligatory upon us in respect to *divine worship*,—such duties as praise, prayer, preaching the gospel, and observing the sacramental ordinances;—and no human authority may either repeal these laws or add to them. But in respect to the duties which we owe to our neighbor, that is, to our fellow-man, in any relation he holds to us or can ever hold; God has left the most of these duties to the authoritative decision of human governments. He has thus made a difference betwixt these two classes of duties. The reason for this difference seems to be this;

namely, man's wisdom can reach farther in ascertaining what is fit or right betwixt him and his fellow-man, than in ascertaining what is fit or right betwixt him and his God: and consequently, man can legislate in respect to property, and other matters of human right, but not in respect to prayer, and other matters of the first class of duties. Moreover, in respect to worship, God is himself one of the parties. The parties are not man and man, as they are in all social duties; but they are man and God:—and therefore, it would seem but fit and natural, that God should legislate *exclusively* in respect to the duties which we owe to *Him*, and more specifically, than in respect to the duties which we owe to one another. Hence, we find it so. Explicit divine law regulates all the *particulars* of the one class of duties; the *particulars* of the other class of duties are left to human law, or the regulations of human society.

But this latter class of duties, that is, our social duties, are *not left* to the *individual* judgment or independent choice of men, in such a sense, that they may obey or disobey human government just as they please. Not in the least. Human government is by the divine will. Obedience to it is obligatory upon men, by the will and law of God. St. Paul directing Titus how to preach, (and therefore directing all ministers of the gospel who come after him,) says to him, "Put them in mind to be subject to principalities and powers, to obey magistrates:" and I am doing it in this sermon. Human government is of divine authority, not the *kind*, but the fact. And consequently, our action about human government, our obedience to it, and our disobedience, are as much matters of religion, and coming under its authority and obligation, as are any other matters. If religion had nothing to do with them, I would have nothing to do with them here. But it *has* something to do with them. Human government is a divine ordinance. It is of divine authority. It is *not* a thing of mere human authority. Our *religion*, therefore, our holiness and final salvation are concerned in our sentiments, principles, and conduct in reference to human government. If God *has* left to men the choice of the *kind* of government they will have, he has *not* left it to their choice whether they will *obey* human government or not. He has commanded that obedience. Human government and law are by the will of God. This is a religious principle. And almost the entire sum of our second class of duties, by the will of God, lies under the regulation of human government. God has himself legislated in respect to the other class of duties. Human government is founded on the revealed will of God.

The different expressions contained in the texts which we have just read in your hearing, place this principle beyond all controversy. Glance at them again. "Put them in mind to be subject to principalities and powers, to obey magistrates." (I am doing so—I am preaching gospel this morning.) "Let every soul be subject unto the higher powers. For there is no power but *of God.* The powers that be, are ordained *of God.* Whosoever, therefore, resisteth the power, resisteth the ordinance *of God.* Rulers are not a terror to good works, but to the evil. Do that which is good, and thou shalt have praise of the same, for he is a minister *of God* to thee for good." We are commanded to be "subject for conscience' sake." Magistrates "are God's ministers."—What could be plainer?—This is *religion*: not politics, but religion. Human government is "ordained of God." Magistrates are "ministers of God," to whom men are commanded to be "subject for conscience' sake."

This, therefore, settles the principle, on which obedience to human government is the religious duty of men. There may be a point where that obedience may justly stop, (a matter which we shall consider soon;) but the great principle before us now is an important one, namely, that human government and Law are things which exist by the will of God, and men are bound to submit to them on that high ground. This is the general rule. This is a *religious* duty; whatever exceptions we may be able to find sometimes, among the diversities of human Law and human condition under it,—or when human Law would interfere with the first class of our duties, which God does not allow it to do. "The powers that be, are ordained of God."

Let it, therefore, be carefully noticed, that no man or body of men has any right to say, that they will be without government, without Law, or that religion has nothing to do with the question of their civil obedience to Law. Such obedience must *be a part* of their religion, or they cannot be Christians. It is a part of the *will and ordinance* of God.

Among politicians and statesmen, the idea of what they call "the social compact" is a very familiar idea, and sometimes figures largely. They mean by this, that there exists between the different members of every civilized and orderly community, a tacit "compact" or agreement, by which each individual tacitly or impliedly consents to surrender some of his natural rights into the hands of the community in general, or the hands of its government, in order to have the power of the community in general, or power of its government protect him in the enjoyment of others of his rights. Thus, they tell us, that each man receives a benefit from the power of society or government, which he could not secure by his individual power, and receives it in return for the individual natural rights, which he surrenders to the general society or government: so that, on the whole, this "compact" between him and the body politic is beneficial to him. For example, he might not be able to defend his farm from the violence of unjust men, who might deprive him of it; and so he procures the aid of civil government to defend it for him, and in return for this benefit he consents that his farm shall be taxed, and consents also to forego his personal right to defend it himself in any manner he could, and let the government defend it for him in their own way. So of all other civil provisions, rights and duties under the civil government. Politicians are accustomed to refer them all to "the social compact."

I do not complain of this idea of a "social compact," when the idea is presented merely as a justification of government, or as an *explanation* of the propriety, necessity and equity of Law. But when it is presented as *the foundation* on which civil government reposes, though it may satisfy a citizen, it ought not at all to satisfy a Christian.

The truth is, there is no such "social compact." The idea is only a fancy. Human government is not founded on any such "social compact" at all. It either exists by force, or it is founded on the will of God, in every case. Its *just* foundation is the will of God. And when men are submitting to human government, they are not to consider themselves as merely carrying out the implied conditions of a "social compact;" but their duty is, to consider themselves as submitting to an *ordinance* of their God and Maker. Human government is of a more high and sacred and solemn character, than the mere idea of a "social compact" would make it. God has something to do with it—much to do with it. His will is the solid foundation on which it rests, (even though at first it may have been established by force,) and every man is religiously bound to regulate his obedience or disobedience to human government on this divinely revealed principle. "The social compact" may be a very good idea to employ for convincing an infidel in respect to the right of Law; but it is too low and loose an idea for a Christian; it falls far below the truth, and below the just solemnity of obligation.

The *necessity* of human Law results very much, if not entirely, from the injustice of mankind. In no age since the fall of Adam, has any considerable body of men been found so just and upright, that civil Law could be dispensed with. The bad would do injustice to the good, if it were not for Law, and those magistrates appointed by Law, who are "a terror to evil doers." Conscience is not effective in the breast of every sinner, and therefore Law must come in, to hinder that injustice, which, without it, would not be hindered by individual conscience, and to compel that righteousness which, without it, individual conscience would fail to enforce. As individual conscience becomes more stringent, civil Law may become more lax. If men would be just towards one another of themselves, there would be no necessity of human Law, to compel them to abstain from injury and to perform their duties to one another.

Consequently, Law is a friend to the human race. It is the protector of the good man; and it punishes the bad man, only for the purpose of securing rights,—property, liberty and life. And even the bad would be worse off a thousand fold than they are, if there were no efficient Law to restrain them by its authority and sanctions.

The *importance* of civil Law is vastly great. Its importance can scarcely be exaggerated by any representation. The most of our earthly happiness lies under the protection of human Law, and lies there by the will of God. We have not an item of property, in land, or houses, or goods, or chattels, or money, which the Law does not guard for us; and we have very little indeed, which we could effectually guard for ourselves. If this protecting, guarding Law is not enforced,—if the Law is obstructed, or crippled, or baffled, or violently set at naught; then, the security of civilized society is gone, and our property, our liberty, our rights, privileges and life, just lie at the mercy of every unjust man, and any violent and excited band of the wicked!—So important to us is the potential dominion and regular administration of Law.

Moreover our very rights in religion, our privilege to have the word of God and read it, to worship God according to the dictates of our own conscience, to preach the gospel and hear it, are rights and privileges, which, in this unjust world, we could not enjoy for a single year, aside from the protection and potential administration of human government.

If this human government, the government of Law, cannot be maintained, therefore, there is nothing on earth valuable to us, which is secure for a single hour! If the Law cannot be enforced, then government is at an end and anarchy reigns, and all is confusion, uncertainty, and violence! Order, civilization, Christianity is not safe!

There is indeed a *limit* to the obedience due to human government. Such government may become, and sometimes does become, so unjust, oppressive, tyrannical, and cruel, as not to answer the designed, and righteous, and beneficial purposes of government for a whole people; and in such a case, it deserves no respect as an ordinance of God, for it is then acting contrary to the will of God and the necessity of society; and the injured and oppressed people may justly rise in rebellion against such a government, and overthrow it, if they can. But, let it be carefully remembered, that any violent resistance is positive rebellion against the government; and either that resistance must be crushed, or the government must be overturned. There is no middle way—there can be none. In such a case the whole authority and power of the government come into direct hostility and conflict with the violence which resists the execution of Law; and government must crush that violence, or that violence must crush the government. A government is at an end, a nullity, when it cannot execute its laws. Let it be carefully remembered also, that violent resistance to Law cannot be justified, when there is no righteous design to overthrow the government itself; for no man owes a *half*-allegiance to government, or can commit a *half*-high-treason; and besides, Law is too important and delicate a thing to have its majesty trifled with, by the wicked nonsense of a *half*-obedience. Let it be carefully remembered also, that violent resistance to Law cannot be justified, when there is no fair prospect of overthrowing the government, and being able to establish a better one. To justify violent resistance to the laws, it is not enough that the government is unjust and its laws unrighteous; it is necessary also, that there should be no good ground to hope for a cessation of that unrighteousness in some peaceful way, and that there should be a prospect of some good to be gained by the resistance, which good shall be worth more than all the labor, and treasure, and strife, and blood, which the revolution shall cost. Let it be carefully remembered, too, that violent resistance on any one point is rebellion on every point, for "he that offendeth in one point is guilty of all:" such resistance is opposition by force to one entire government—is just a conflict with the powers that be; so that any resisting individual or number of individuals who commence a violent resistance on any one point, have cast off their allegiance to the entire government, and stand in the attitude of open and hostile rebellion.

It may not be an easy thing to settle the right of rebellion—to determine the question, when a people have a right forcibly to resist the execution of regularly enacted Law. But we *can* tell *something* about it. There are some things perfectly clear on this point.

1. To justify rebellion, (or what is the same thing, forcible resistance of the laws,) a government must be so bad, as to manifestly fail of its just end, that is, to promote the happiness of the people. If it does promote that general happiness, it answers the just end of government—it is a good government, and ought not to be overthrown.

2. To justify rebellion, the injustice or failure of a government must be so great, that it cannot be endured,—so great, that it will manifestly be better on the whole, to run all the risks of a bloody conflict, of civil war, than to endure the execution of the governmental laws.

3. To justify rebellion, there must be little or no prospect that the government can be peaceably altered, as ours may be, or that the injustice or oppression of the government can be made to cease by any peaceable means. Violence against government, rebellion, civil war, are no small matters. They bring horrid evils along with them. The injury of government must be very great to justify the introduction of such evils; and if the injury can be made to cease by any peaceable means and within any reasonable time, it would be better to bear the injury for a while, than to involve the nation in confusion and blood, with uncertainty as

to *the result.*—The last four years' experience of nations in Europe may read us a lesson.

A republic is different from a despotism. A nation where a Constitution forming the foundation of Law, limiting its enactments and establishing courts, is plainly written out in language that everybody can understand,—where Constitution and Law provide for their own amendment at the will of the sovereign people expressed in a regular and solemn manner,—where the will of the people thus governs, and (for example,) there is no "taxation without representation," —where the elective franchise is free, and every man capable of intelligently exercising the right may give his voice for altering the Constitution or Law,—and where, therefore, there can be no necessity of violently opposing the laws, and no excuse for meanly evading them;—*such* a nation is very differently conditioned from what it would be, if the will of one man or of a few governed. In such a nation, rebellion, or any evasion of Law, becomes a more serious moral evil. Rebellion *there* can scarcely be called for; and it were difficult to gauge the dimensions of its unrighteousness!

4. To justify rebellion, it is necessary that there should be a fair prospect of successful resistance—of an overthrow of the government. If the resistance is not likely to be successful for good, but is only likely to cost the lives of the resisting individuals and others; then, such individuals are sacrificing themselves and others for no good purpose,—which is a thing that cannot be justified to reason or religion. A man has no right to fling away his life for a mere sentiment, and leave his wife a widow, or his gray-haired parents

without a son to solace them. There must be some fair prospect of great good to come from it, before one can justly fling his life into the scale, in a violent contest with the government.

5. To justify rebellion, there must be a fair prospect of the firm *establishment of a better government*, and the enactment of more just laws, after the present government is overturned. Nothing can justify a revolution, a conflict, a waste of treasure and blood, which are not going *to gain anything* in the end.—Again, the last four years' experience of European nations may read us a lesson.

6. To justify rebellion, or what is the same thing, violent resistance to the execution of the laws, it is necessary that something more than a *small fraction* of the people should rise in such a resistance. If the people in general are ready for it, and are willing to run all the hazards of a rebellious conflict with the government, conscious that they have righteousness and the God of righteousness on their side; this is a very different affair from what it would be, if only a minority of the people were ready for rebellion. Such a minority have no right, on account of their deemed injuries, to plunge the nation into a civil war, for the purpose of overturning a government which suits the great mass of the people;—a civil war, in which there is every prospect, that the government and the majority who aim to support it will prevail; and prevailing, must crush their hostile opponents, this hasty and reckless minority.

These are some of the things which appear necessary, in order to justify violent resistance of Law. They must *all* exist, or such resistance would be criminal,—contrary to reason, to benevolence, and to Christ.

It is not a thing to be expected at all among mankind, that all laws should be right, or "just and equal." Human legislation must be expected to bear the marks of an imperfection, which attaches itself to everything human. If obedience to government were obligatory, only on the condition that all the laws of that government are just; then, such obedience would mean nothing at all, and every man would be absolved from all allegiance to the government, and from all obligations to obey. Such is man, so limited his wisdom and so imperfect his holiness, that human laws must necessarily be imperfect, and must, therefore, necessarily operate hardly in some instances, upon more or less of the people. It is impossible, that the thing should be otherwise —in the very nature of the case, it is impossible. And if every individual were allowed to be the judge in his own case, whether or not the law operated so hardly upon him that he might disobey; *then* his *obligation* to obedience would mean just nothing at all, and Law would be nothing more to him than mere advice. It might be very good advice, but he might spurn it, if he chose. *I* may think it hard and unjust upon myself, that, in the great "Empire State," by a sort of "bill of attainder," (I know not what else to call it,—I suppose I must not call it a *slave law*,) I am prohibited from holding any "office of profit or trust," because I *will preach* the gospel, and people will hear me;—but notwithstanding this law, (which you will not allow me to call by any hard name,) you think me under obligation to obey the government,—and I think so too. I shall not rebel.

The *execution* of the Law also, must necessarily be imperfect, for the same great reason—human imperfection: judges and jurors are not infallible. But, what then? *God knew all this* when he ordained human government, and commanded us to be subject to it. Such government, with all its unavoidable imperfection and errors, on the whole is beneficial—indispensable—we could not do without it.—And rarely, very rarely indeed, is there a single instance of an individual man, here or beyond the Potomac, whom Law has injured *more* than it has benefited. Even if that Law unjustly takes away his liberty or his life, it may have done him more good than injury; his liberty or his life might have been sooner and more cruelly destroyed without it. It would be hard to prove the contrary, in any one case that ever existed or ever will, here or elsewhere.

The best and wisest Laws ever enacted by man, or that ever will be enacted by man, may sometimes operate hardly, even destructively, upon some particular persons. An innocent man may be accused of murder, tried, convicted, and sentenced to ignominious execution. But, *what then?* May this man, who *knows* his innocence, justly arm himself with deadly weapons, and kill the officer who would execute the sentence of the Law upon him,—and thus get out of his hands? May this innocent man's neighbors, who know his innocence as well as he, "*lawfully interpose their own persons*" betwixt him and the officer of Law, and thus rescue him?—and may they do this, because they have decided for themselves, that this is not a case "*where the administration of justice is concerned*"? If so, then all Law and Government must soon come to an end, and anarchy, mobs and confusion reign! If so, then each man becomes really his own Lawmaker, and when *he thinks* the Law unjust towards him, may resist it unto blood! If one man is at liberty to "*be fully prepared for* his own defense," and calling the legal officer an "assailant," or an "assassin," may resist the execution of one law which he deems hard upon him, then another man may do the same thing in reference to another law; and the consequence inevitably must be, that all Government, Law and security are at end! If my neighbor may arm *himself*, and kill a legal officer who attempts the discharge of his sworn duty; then I may arm *myself* also, when I deem the Law unjust to me, and kill another legal officer, who attempts to execute the Law! And if all this may be, LAW is nothing but a bugbear or a bubble—is a dead letter—and the texts of God's word which we have just read to you may be disobeyed, and ought to be blotted from the Bible!

My brethren, this is a very solemn subject! No theme of earth could be more so. All our earthly benefits, and no small part of our spiritual privileges and hopes are wrapped up in it. Religion *cannot* prosper, if Law is not potential—if the minds of the people are to be perpetually agitated, distracted and tormented, by confusion, fear and uncertainty!

---

I have stated these great principles, and made these general remarks upon the subject presented in our texts, on account of some recent teachings which have been put forth as *religious*—put forth in *religious* publications, by *ministers* of the gospel. I have no reference to mere politics—to political papers or political parties, whig or democrat. I have never entered into such matters: other things occupy me. I have never given but one vote in any legal election, during the eighteen years I have resided in the State since I returned to it; and I never expect to give another. And if principles opposite to those I have laid down in this sermon were promulgated among us, only by politicians and political parties and papers, I should not advert to them here. I have always supposed, that some extravagant and evil principles would be occasionally promulgated for party purposes and political effect, and that the people very well understand this, and therefore will not be led very far astray by them. And whenever such evil principles have been put forth in the name of religion, by men whose fanatical phrensy contemned the Sabbath and other institutions of God, (like some of our Northern fanatics, "men of one idea" and not capable of two,) I have very seldom adverted to them at all, but have supposed it best to leave them to be counteracted by their own extravagance and by the character of their advocates, and let them die by their own contemptibility. But now, principles, contrary to the plain meaning of the texts before us, come to our ears from some more respectable quarters, and in the name of religion. I should be a traitor to the high trust of this pulpit, if I did not caution you against them. Forbearance and delicacy must sometimes have limits. We owe duties to truth and Christianity, which tenderness must not make us violate.

The "New York Evangelical Congregational Association" recently passed the following Resolution in respect to the "Fugitive-Slave Law,"—a Law regularly enacted by the Congress of the United States:—

"Resolved, That we cannot recognize this Law, as of any binding force upon the citizens of our country."—(I am thankful that these modest men did not go on, like him of the triple crown, to absolve "the citizens of our country" from all allegiance to the government, and give our rulers over into the hands of a majesty fit to take careof them.)

A *religious* paper, edited by Congregational clergymen, holding respectable stations, Pastors of churches,—a paper professedly devoted to the cause of Christ,—holds the following language in an *Editorial* article, under the caption, "How to oppose the Fugitive-Slave Law":—

This *religious* paper says,—"To the fugitives themselves . . . this Law is no Law . . . and to resist it even unto death, is their right, and it may be their duty . . . . . To each *individual* fugitive, to every man or woman, who having escaped from bondage and tasted liberty, is in hourly peril of being seized and dragged back to slavery, we say,—Be fully prepared for your own defense. If to you death seems better than slavery, then refuse not to die—whether on the way-side, at your own threshold, or even as a felon upon the gallows. Defend your liberty and the liberty of your wife and children, as you would defend your life and theirs against the assassin. If you die thus, you die nobly, and your blood shall be the redemption of your race. Should you destroy the life of your assailant, you will pass into the custody of the criminal Law. . . . . . . under an indictment for murder; but the verdict of the community, and the verdict of almost any jury will be, justifiable homicide in self-defense . . . . Or should a different verdict be found, and you be condemned to die as a murderer, your ignominious death shall be luminous with the halo of a martyr, and your sacrifice shall be for the deliverance of your people."

Such are the *religious* principles, and such is the *religious* advice of these *religious* ministers!

I am sorry to see this. *I never read more wicked and abominable principles!* They deserve not only the reprehension of every christian, but the entire indignation of *all civilized mankind!* They advise private arming with bloody weapons—they advise violent resistance and murder—the murder of officers of civil Law engaged in the discharge of the duty which they have sworn to perform! I have no words to express my abhorrence of these wicked and outrageous sentiments, so directly contrary to the whole nature of all civilized society, to the precepts of the Bible, and the whole spirit of Christianity! I speak not of the *men*. Good men may err. But these principles, which these ministers have published as religious ones, are horribly and outrageously wicked!

There are other things in this religious paper, which we think are calculated to do immense mischief. This editorial article "would utter its remonstrance against all violent resistance to the execution of the Law." Indeed! Very quiet and peaceful, after having talked about being "fully prepared for defense"—about death "on the wayside, at the threshold and on the gallows"—about "murder," and about "martyrdom." Away with such morality! aiming at one thing and professing another!—"If one sees a fellow man struggling with his captors, . . . . . he may lawfully interpose his own person between the parties and separate them." Away with such morality! encouraging people to "act a lie," by opposing Law while professing to obey it! And this species of morality is virtually commended to the jury-box; and its inmates are furnished in advance with a verdict here prepared for their use—"justifiable homicide in self-defense"! Away with such morality! encouraging a juror to violate his oath, by disregarding the Law, which he has just sworn to his country and to his God, shall govern his verdict! and encouraging a fugitive to expect him to do so!—We may yet see whether the jurymen of our country will regard their oath, or will follow the religious counsel of this religious paper.

I am not justifying slavery. I am pleading obedience to the texts before me. Slavery may be wrong. Be it so; there is still a *righteous* method to get rid of it. But if slavery *is* wrong, that does not make violence and murder *right*.

I am not justifying the fugitive-slave Law. It may be wrong: it may be unwise and unconstitutional. I think that any wise and modest man would hesitate much to pronounce it unconstitutional, after its enactment by a body of men who *aimed* to abide by the constitution, and who studied the matter most intensely, with every opportunity for information and with minds trained for years in the depths of legal science. But, be it wrong—be it unwise and unconstitutional; there are civil courts to decide upon its constitutionality, and no man has *any right* to decide for *himself* that it is unconstitutional, and act upon that decision: if he had such a right, then every man would be his own Lawmaker, and public Constitution and Law would be nothing but a bugbear or a bubble! Be it wrong; there is a peaceful, prescribed way of amending both Law and Constitution,—and a wrong in the Law does not make false-swearing by the juryman and murder by the fugitive *right!*

It is a most marvellous thing, what a number of clergymen north of Mason and Dixon's line, have, all of a sudden, become such great *Constitutional lawyers!* Never before was anything like it! It is a modern miracle! A decision upon a great constitutional question is nothing to them! How amazingly these profound legalists, these clergyman jurists, would adorn the high courts of the country, if they would only consent to take their seat upon the bench! The Judges of the United States Supreme Court ought to be thankful, that these clergymen Judges have done their duty for them in advance, deciding the law to be unconstitutional, and no more is to be done! Benevolent men, these clergymen! Some have done the duty of the jurors for them, and others the duty of the judges—the verdict and the decision are both recorded! yea indeed, in advance, and without pay!

But seriously, it were far better, that these clergymen should attend to their own appropriate duties to which their Master has bidden them, than to be engaged in fostering excitements among their people, which *never can* result in any good, civil or religious. If we shall have the rebellion, disunion, and civil war, to which these evil principles and these excitements tend, the guilt of such clergymen will not be small! I would not have their accountability for all the gold of Ophir!

But it is not all the clergymen of this part of the country, nor the most of them, nor the half of them, who have turned Constitutional lawyers, or turned law opposers. I hesitate not to say, it is only a small minority, and those in general who are not entitled to the most respect for erudition, sense, or excellence of character. The (New School) Synod of New York and New Jersey, as respectable a body of ministers and elders as is to be found in the Presbyterian Church, at their late meeting in this city, had good sense enough, and good religion enough, to "leave the constitutionality of the recent enactment" (the Fugitive Slave Law) "to be adjudicated by the civil tribunals of the country." They deserve the thanks of the country and of all mankind. The solid sense and real religion of the land will respect their decision.

I have nothing to do with politics or party. I am only insisting upon religious obedience to Law. I am preaching the texts before me. Such obedience is a religious duty.

It is the will of God. I appeal to the texts. They proclaim the Law of God. Peaceful subjection to government *is* his law; and men are guilty of sophistry and falsehood, when, to excuse wicked evasion of Law or violent resistance, they pretend to appeal to what they call "the higher laws of God." *There are no such higher laws.* The texts before me are his law. If one man has a moral right, either cunningly to evade or openly to violate Law, under such pleading, then another man has the same right to violate *another* Law; and thus any villainy on earth may be perpetrated under the sacred names of "conscience," and "the higher laws of God!" Nothing is *safe* in the hands of men of such principles. These principles undermine the foundations *of all society among men!* As I told you last Wednesday evening in my lecture, the question before the country is *not*, (as the deceivers pretend,) whether God's laws are not higher than man's, or whether God's laws are to be obeyed. Nobody disputes either of these things. Nobody ever did. But the question is, whether it is the will of God that men should submit to the laws of the land, or aim to paralyze law, cheat it, cripple it, resist it, and thus overthrow the government of the country—a government at this moment more beneficial than any other that ever existed.

Nor is it true, that the fugitive slave is made an "outlaw," and on *that* ground justifiable for bloody and murderous resistance of Law. He is under the protection of Law; and if any man injures him or kills him, the Law will avenge him, just as soon as it would you or me. He is *not* made an outlaw: common sense knows better.

The matter before us is a very serious matter. The wicked principles of which I have spoken, disguise it as you will, tend directly to anarchy, confusion, and civil war! The question *is not*, whether slavery is right, or the Fugitive Slave Law right. It draws deeper. The question is, shall Law be put in force, and the government of the country stand; or shall Law be resisted, and the government of the country disobeyed, and the nation plunged into all the horrors of civil war? If Law cannot be executed, it is time to write the epitaph of your country!

Suffer me to utter a few words of earnest counsel to you, my beloved people.

1. Beware of the influence of *mere feeling* on this serious subject. Your feelings may be with the slave,—so are mine, so are those of most of the Southern people. We all want men to be free; and *no more* do we want it now, than did the inhabitants of this country before we were born: the extravagant fanaticism and noisy zeal of the Northern abolitionists have not increased the sentiment of the country in favour of freedom a single item. But what can we *do?* This is a very grave and difficult subject. One thing is certain,—the perpetual abuse of our Southern brethren, violence, disunion, and bloody murder will do us no good,—whether we are bondmen or freemen. And when we think on this subject, let us aim to be cool, unimpassioned, deliberate, and give reason and religion their just influence over us.

2. Beware of prejudice. Do not make up your mind hastily, and under the impulses of mere feeling, without

any just and extensive information. Study the matter calmly, extensively, and on all sides and aspects of it.

3. Study it *religiously*. Keep it, in your mind, aloof from all the excitements and influences of party and party spirit. Let me say to you, my beloved people, study it on your knees, in earnest prayer to God. Learn your duty from God's word, praying in the Holy Ghost.

4. Aim to cultivate the entire spirit of your Lord and Master, Jesus Christ. Feel as he felt. Act as he acted. Pray as he prayed. Seek the *salvation* of sinners, as he sought it,—evidently putting more value upon *that* for every dying son of Adam, than upon all things earthly. Oh remember, you *will be the best citizens, just when you are the best Christians*;—and I do believe in my heart, you will do most earthly good to your fellow-men, just when you do them most spiritual good,—leading them, by example, by precept, and prayer, to "seek *first* the kingdom of God."

5. Be obedient to the laws of your land. Do not resist these *ordinances of God*. Stand by the Constitution of your country. If that die, *the most* of your happiness and your hopes die with it!—yea, it would be a calamity to the civilized world! Christianity herself would be hindered a whole century in her march! Respect your rulers. Frown indignantly upon the low and vile abuse now heaped so liberally upon the great men of your country. Be peaceful citizens. Be a *law-abiding people*, with all your sentiments opposed to violence, bloodshed, and confusion; and aim to allay all the excited and angry feelings that may come up around you.

Finally; have your hope and your trust in God. Men women, and children, I beseech every one of you to beware of the spirit of worldliness, and the excitements of worldly subjects and interests; and let not such interests and subjects prevent your conversion to Christ, your holiness and eternal salvation. Pray for yourselves, your children, your rulers; and let your prayerful and humble trust in God hold you safe, amid all the agitations of a world that you must soon leave for another. God grant it to you, through Jesus Christ our Saviour. Amen.

www.ingramcontent.com/pod-product-compliance
Lightning Source LLC
LaVergne TN
LVHW011132110826
845150LV00008B/2300
* 9 7 8 1 4 1 8 1 9 4 0 6 2 *